GUARDING
NUCLEAR WEAPONS FACILITIES

BY JILL SHERMAN

Published by The Child's World®
1980 Lookout Drive • Mankato, MN 56003-1705
800-599-READ • www.childsworld.com

Acknowledgments
The Child's World®: Mary Swensen, Publishing Director
Red Line Editorial: Editorial direction and production
The Design Lab: Design

Design Element: Iaroslav Neliubov/Shutterstock Images
Photographs ©: U.S. Navy, cover, 1; Bettmann/Corbis, 5; U.S.
Department of Energy, 7; SuperStock/Corbis, 10; Adam Brimer/Knoxville
News Sentinel/AP Images, 12; Erik Schelzig/AP Images, 13; Corbis, 15;
Seth Wenig/AP Images, 16; AP Images, 19, 21; Tobias Hase/EPA/Corbis,
20

ISBN 9781503808133
LCCN 2015958277

Printed in the United States of America
Mankato, MN
June, 2016
PA02302

ABOUT THE AUTHOR

Jill Sherman lives and writes in Brooklyn,
New York. She has written more than a
dozen books for young readers. She enjoys
researching new topics.

TABLE OF CONTENTS

CHAPTER 1

Secret Development

A **nuclear** bomb is dropped. It **detonates**. There is a loud, bright explosion and a huge cloud of smoke. Then there is rubble and death.

Nuclear weapons get their power from reactions. These reactions take place in atoms. Atoms are microscopic. But they can release huge power. An atom's center is its nucleus. When the nuclei of some atoms split, it is called nuclear fission. When certain nuclei combine, it is called nuclear fusion.

These reactions cause releases of energy. This energy comes in the form of huge explosions and clouds of smoke. The reactions also create **radioactive** material.

Nuclear weapons get power from these reactions. The most common atoms used in nuclear weapons come from the elements plutonium and uranium.

An atomic bomb production facility in Tennessee in 1945

The first **atomic** bombs were created in secret. World War II started in 1939. It involved many powerful nations. Japan, Germany, and Italy led a side called the Axis powers. France, the United Kingdom, and other countries formed the Allies. Dozens of countries were involved.

That year, the U.S. government got a letter. It was from European scientists, including Albert Einstein. It warned that the Germans were building a giant bomb. The bomb, if successful, could kill many people. Then the Japanese attacked Pearl Harbor in 1941. The United States joined the war. The U.S. government needed a new weapon.

So the U.S. government started the highly secretive Manhattan Project. It was so secret that even Harry S. Truman did not know it existed when he became president. The Manhattan Project had a few goals. One was to research atomic bombs. Another was to build them.

More than 120,000 people were involved. Some workers did not know what they were working on. They were not allowed to talk about the Manhattan Project. They signed documents promising to keep their work a secret. All mail was reviewed. Some of it was **censored**.

This was done to keep information from enemy spies. Discussion among workers was limited. People only knew what they needed to know to do their jobs. That way nobody could give away the project's secrets.

There were sites in several countries. Some were in the United States. Others were in the United Kingdom. There were some in Canada,

MANHATTAN PROJECT SITES IN THE UNITED STATES

too. The project was secret. Sites were placed in hidden areas.

The main facility was in Los Alamos, New Mexico. People needed security passes to get in. There were security checkpoints. There were tall fences around the base topped with barbed wire. Guards kept watch at all hours.

The security started before people even began working. Federal Bureau of Investigation (FBI) background checks were done before hires. Employees got a badge. It had their photo and job title on it. The badge also showed a security clearance. Security inside Los Alamos was a team effort. The FBI, Army, Navy, and the U.S. Treasury Department were all involved.

The Manhattan Project built two nuclear bombs. The first was called Little Boy. The second was named Fat Man. The plutonium in Fat Man was man-made. But the uranium in Little Boy was rare. So no test detonations were done. Nobody was sure how powerful Little Boy really was.

In 1945, President Harry S. Truman made the tough decision

MANHATTAN PROJECT SITE SIGNS

There were always reminders of how important secrecy was at Manhattan Project sites. The work relied on it. There were signs around the work sites. Some said, "What you see here / what you do here / what you hear here / when you leave here / Let it stay here." Others said, "Loose talk helps our enemy, so let's keep our trap shut!"

to use the Manhattan Project weapons to end World War II. Truman asked Japanese leaders to surrender. They did not.

On August 6, 1945, Little Boy was dropped on Nagasaki, Japan. Truman again urged the Japanese to surrender. They refused. On August 9, Fat Man was released on Hiroshima. Japan surrendered six days later. World War II was officially over.

The two bombs did a ton of damage. Nearly everything within a mile (1.6 km) of the Hiroshima drop site was destroyed. In Nagasaki, nearly everything within a half mile (.8 km) was destroyed.

Many died from the explosions. But there was also **radiation** from the bombs. The radiation led to thousands of deaths within three weeks. Even those that did not die were not safe. The radiation went on to cause cancer, blindness, and other symptoms in the coming decades. It affected generations of families.

The Manhattan Project changed the world and ended a costly war. But the bombs killed thousands.

The atomic bomb dropped on Hiroshima, seen here, killed thousands but helped bring an end to World War II.

It is believed around 200,000 people died because of the bombs. The world saw their power. Since the 1940s, nuclear weapons have gotten even more powerful. The security around them has, too.

CHAPTER 2

Control Systems

Nuclear facilities have layers of security. The first levels are physical barriers. These include walls and fences. Guards patrol these areas. But they are not the only ones keeping watch. There are cameras, too. And motion sensors are always alert. They track movement in sensitive areas.

Everybody who enters these facilities goes through tight surveillance. But the process is not perfect. Some activists have gotten in and hung banners protesting nuclear weapons.

There are safety measures to prevent the weapons, also

BREAK-IN AT Y-12

The Y-12 National Security Complex is in Oak Ridge, Tennessee. Uranium is produced and stored for nuclear weapons there. Three protesters broke into the facility on July 28, 2012. They cut their way through fences and reached an area holding uranium. The intruders hung banners. They also spray-painted the walls. They were protesting nuclear weapons. They wanted to show that the weapons are not as safe as they could be. The protesters were sent to prison.

Michael Walli (left) and Sister Megan Rice were two of the three protesters that broke into the Y-12 facility in July 2012.

known as nukes, from going off when they are not supposed to. One measure is control systems that can keep weapons from detonating if stolen or damaged. Another measure is a special area called an isolation barrier. Electric shocks and fire could damage the devices. Their insides are protected in an isolation barrier to stop such damage from taking place. It is separate from detonators.

Dangerous types of uranium and plutonium are produced around the United States at plants such as the Y-12 complex.

Some devices also have a fire-resistant pit. It is hard. The pit holds the dangerous material found within a nuclear weapon. Pits keep this material from spreading in case there is a fire.

Atomic weapons can destroy entire cities. That is why they are built with such care. The safety measures protect the weapon, its handlers, and the public in case of an accident.

CHAPTER 3

Weapon Locks

The insides of nuclear weapons are secure. So are the outsides. **Casings** can withstand shocks, fire, and impact. This helps ensure weapons go off at the right time.

There are also locks on the weapons. Scientists used to use mechanical combination locks. Now, most nuclear weapons are locked with a permissive action link (PAL). A PAL needs two different codes. Two people must enter them. This is important. It makes it impossible to enter the codes to launch a nuclear weapon alone.

Locks and codes also stop fake data from being sent to the weapon. Criminals try to gain access to launch system computers to send this fake data. This is called spoofing. Spoofing could set off devices at the wrong time.

The weapons have a system. The system reads the codes. Once the codes are received, the device

The casing of a Mark-17 thermonuclear weapon

is ready to fire. But it does not explode right away. It needs to reach its target first. There are sensors on the weapon that help with this. They measure the device's speed and movement. They also measure temperature and pressure. This data creates a signal. The signal needs to be correct for the bomb to go off.

Nuclear weapons can do major damage. None have been used since the bombs dropped on Nagasaki and Hiroshima. Safety systems help make using them safer.

Keeping official nuclear bombs safe is one thing. But terrorists try to make their own weapons.

Tools such as these were used to measure radioactive material and intercept dirty bombs after the September 11, 2001, terrorist attacks.

Sometimes these groups try to make dirty bombs. Dirty bombs combine normal explosives with radioactive material. If a dirty bomb explodes, that radioactive material can spread throughout the area of the explosion. Governments need to know more about these devices. So they have built dirty bombs themselves. Then they have detonated them. This helps governments learn how to deal with the danger.

SUITCASE NUKES

Terrorists often try to make new weapons. One example is a suitcase nuke. It is also called a backpack nuke. A suitcase nuke is a portable nuclear **warhead**. It can be carried and detonated by a single person. Suitcase nukes are expensive to create. Some U.S. soldiers used to carry suitcase nukes on their backs. Fortunately they never used them.

CHAPTER 4

Fear of a Nuclear Firestorm

Nuclear weapons are a big part of defense systems. Today, many countries have nuclear weapons. Most countries do not want to use them. Most have these weapons as **deterrents**. Countries are less likely to attack knowing other countries also have nuclear weapons.

Countries with nuclear weapons know the power of these weapons. The explosions in Japan showed how dangerous nuclear weapons are. So countries with nukes work together. They try to keep the world safe from nuclear warfare.

Much has been learned from nuclear test sites. Scientists have studied areas affected by nuclear weapons. The scientists have sifted through rubble. This helps them learn more about the devices' power. Scientists have also measured burn marks. This determines the height of nuclear fireballs.

In addition, scientists have examined nuclear attack survivors. Different countries have shared this information with one another. There are different parts of attacks that affect people. These include **shock waves** and radiation poisoning.

Nuclear detonations cause damage in stages. Weapons are detonated at a certain height. This allows for the most impact. Explosions create sudden changes in air pressure. These are called shock waves. These can destroy buildings. Then there is a blast of nuclear wind that travels close to 300 miles (483 km) per second.

THE COLD WAR

The Cold War started in the 1940s. Some believe it lasted into the 1980s. Others say it stretched to the 1990s. The two main countries involved were the United States and the U.S.S.R. The U.S.S.R. later became Russia. It is called the Cold War because the countries did not actually fight each other directly. Each had powerful nuclear weapons. If one side launched a nuke, the other would also. Both countries would be destroyed. This is known as mutually assured destruction. Instead, the United States and U.S.S.R. helped support other countries that fought for the causes the two larger nations believed in.

The damage from the Nagasaki bombing, seen here, and the damage done in Hiroshima have made countries hesitant to use nuclear weapons.

The weapon also flashes light and heat. This light is very bright. It can temporarily blind anyone looking directly at it. This is called flash blindness. The heat is intense. Everything it touches can catch fire. Even people several miles away are not safe. They can still feel the effects of the light and heat.

Nuclear radiation is released when the weapon detonates. The radiation acts like tiny invisible bullets. These are gamma rays. They pass through nearly everything. Nuclear radiation is deadly and causes radiation sickness. Symptoms include sores,

Large countries such as the United States and Russia often
work together to prevent the use of nuclear weapons.

fever, fatigue, nausea, hair and blood loss, fainting,
cancer, and more. The sickness can be treated.
Medication and blood transfusions help. Antibiotics
are also used to fight infections.

There are also secondary effects. The radiation
fills particles around the blast. These particles are
called fallout. They settle back into the blast area.
These particles are dangerous. They can also cause
radiation sickness.

Nuclear fallout can take many forms. Sometimes
radiated pieces of debris can fall into bodies of
water. This can pollute drinking supplies. Other

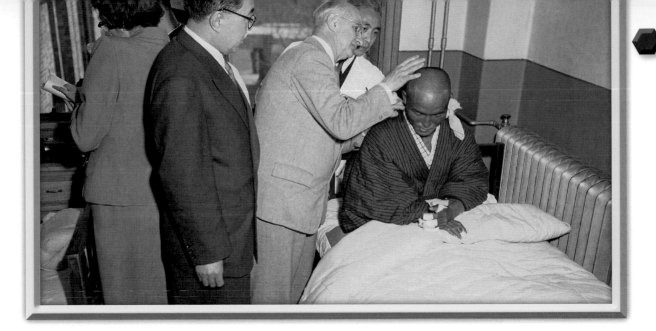

A man is examined for radioactive fallout symptoms after a nuclear test in March 1954.

times radiation can seep into the ground. This can poison food growing in the area.

Wind and rain can increase the damage and add to the danger. One example was when Little Boy was dropped on Nagasaki. There was intense wind. It spread fire around the city. There were tornadoes of flame. This made it hard for help to reach the city.

The nuclear weapons that exist now are more powerful than ever. The world would be in grave danger if they fell into the wrong hands. That is why countries must guard them carefully.

GLOSSARY

atomic (uh-TAHM-ik) Something that is atomic has to do with tiny particles called atoms. Atomic bombs were developed as part of the Manhattan Project.

casings (KAY-sings) Casings are the outer shells of nuclear weapons. The casings of nuclear weapons are built to withstand outside forces that can cause accidental detonation.

censored (SEN-surd) Something is censored when it has had parts removed, often in an effort to keep secrets. Documents at Manhattan Project sites were often censored to keep sensitive information out of the hands of enemy spies.

deterrents (dih-TUR-uhnts) Deterrents are things that discourage actions. Nuclear weapons are deterrents to attacks because countries do not want to start a nuclear war.

detonates (DET-uh-nayts) An item blows up when it detonates. An atomic bomb causes tons of damage when it detonates.

nuclear (NOO-klee-ur) Nuclear items work off energy that is created when tiny particles called atoms are split apart or joined together. Nuclear weapons get their power from small chemical reactions that lead to huge damage.

radiation (ray-dee-AY-shun) Radiation is energy made up of tiny microscopic particles. Nuclear radiation can cause damage by getting inside water, soil, and human bodies.

radioactive (ray-dee-oh-AK-tiv) Radioactive materials emit radiation. Dirty bombs are a combination of standard explosive materials and radioactive material.

shock waves (SHOK WAYVS) Shock waves are bursts of high air pressure often caused by an explosion. Shock waves are one of the major effects of atomic bombs.

warhead (WAWR-hed) A warhead is the explosive part of a nuclear weapon. A suitcase nuke is a weapon with a smaller, portable warhead.

TO LEARN MORE

IN THE LIBRARY

Bodden, Valerie. *The Bombing of Hiroshima and Nagasaki*.
Mankato, MN: Creative Education and Creative Paperbacks, 2016.

Fetter-Vorm, Jonathan. *Trinity: A Graphic History of the
First Atomic Bomb*. New York: Hill and Wang, 2013.

Sheinkin, Steve. *Bomb: The Race to Build—and Steal—the
World's Most Dangerous Weapon*. New York: Flash Point, 2012.

ON THE WEB

Visit our Web site for links about guarding nuclear
weapons facilities: **childsworld.com/links**

*Note to Parents, Teachers, and Librarians: We routinely verify
our Web links to make sure they are safe and active sites.
So encourage your readers to check them out!*

INDEX